The 5 Biggest Improvements Advertisers Can Make

(Breakthrough the Marketing Clutter <u>NOW</u>)

davidpetro | consulting

"Successful and unsuccessful people do not vary greatly in their abilities. They vary in their desire to reach their potential."
-John Maxwell-

The 5 Biggest Improvements Advertisers Can Make

(Breakthrough the Marketing Clutter <u>NOW</u>)

David Petro

1st Edition – 2015
2nd Edition – 2023

Published by
David Petro Consulting

Cover Design and Illustration Layout
David Petro

davidpetro|consulting

The 5 Biggest Improvements Advertisers Can Make
(Breakthrough the Marketing Clutter <u>NOW</u>)

David Petro

Copyright 2015, 2023 by David Petro

davidpetro|consulting

The 5 Biggest Improvements Advertisers Can Make

(Breakthrough the Marketing Clutter <u>NOW</u>)

Corresponds with the book:
The 5 Biggest Mistakes Advertisers Make
(Breakthrough the Marketing Clutter)

CONTENTS

davidpetro|consulting

Section 1: Correcting the First Mistake
The Guide to Identifying Your Ideal Customer
Corresponds with Chapter IV

Are you exactly the same consumer as the people in your surrounding community? While you may live in the same neighborhood, and in comparable homes, does this really make you the same type of consumer? Did you buy identical vehicles, television sets and furniture? Do you vacation in the same places? Attend the same church, or shop at the same grocery store, buying the same food?
Of course the answer to all of these questions is no. But look how quickly I can separate your interests from those of your closest neighbors and friends. Now, imagine how dissimilar your customers can be.

It is no longer acceptable to identify your business's consumer demographic as Adults 18-plus or Women 25 to 54 years of age. It's just not enough information to work with. While age demographics can be a good starting point, they certainly cannot be the be-all, end-all. Age demographics only give you a small glimpse at who you are marketing to. You must look deeper into who your customers really are. What makes up their unique wants and needs?

The following section is designed to help you segment your entire customer base.

Total Percentage of Prospective Male Consumers:
(Ages 12 to 65+)

Total Percentage of Prospective Female Consumers:
(Ages 12 to 65+)

Total Percentage of Caucasian Consumers:

Total Percentage of African American Consumers:

Total Percentage of Latino Consumers:

Total Percentage of Asian American Consumers:

Age Cell Groups by Percentage:

6 to 12: _____

13 to 17: _____

18 to 24: _____

25 to 34: _____

35 to 44: _____

45 to 54: _____

55 to 64: _____

65+: _____

Question 1: Who are your *core* consumers?

(Who is the consumer group that makes or breaks your business?)

Age: _____

Gender: _____

Ethnicity: _____

Marital Status: _____

Household Income: _____

Occupation: _____

Geographic Residence: _____

Type of Residence: _____

Education: _____

Family/Number of Children: _____

Type of Vehicle(s) likely to Own: _____

Travel/Recreational Interest: _____

Hobbies: _____

Fitness: _____

Political Affiliation: _____

Religion/Spiritual: _____

Additional Information: _____

Question 2: Who is your _secondary_ consumer group?
(Who is the next consumer group that makes buying decisions?)
Age: _____
Gender: _____
Ethnicity: _____
Marital Status: _____
Household Income: _____
Occupation: _____
Geographic Residence: _____
Type of Residence: _____
Education: _____
Family/Number of Children: _____
Type of Vehicle(s) likely to Own: _____
Travel/Recreational Interest: _____
Hobbies: _____
Fitness: _____
Political Affiliation: _____
Religion/Spiritual: _____
Additional Information: _____

By charting your consumer audience in this manner, you will be equipped with vital marketing information. You will have a greater understanding of who your ideal customers are, what they look like, and how to find them.

Keep in mind; you may not need to discover all the information listed above. But the more you know about your ideal customers, the easier it will be to create an effective marketing campaign.

HINT: There is a quick way to accumulate much of your ideal customer's psychographic data. Many of your local media outlets such as radio, television and print companies use software programs that provides them with qualitative information. (Remember: If you ask the right questions, you'll receive the right answers). Or, you can always ask for a little help. I can assemble a thorough qualitative consumer report on your industry for you.

PERSONAL NOTES

Section 2: Correcting the Second Mistake

The Guide to Creating an Effective Message

Corresponds with Chapter V

All too frequently, advertisers miss the mark when it comes to creating the right message. A well-crafted message will engage the audience. It will grab the consumer's attention and inspire action.

Before you can create an amazing advertising message, you must first know what your target consumers are seeking. You can achieve this by uncovering the needs and wants of your ideal customers.

There are five key elements that must be addressed in order to identify your ideal customer's requirements and create a motivating marketing campaign.

Four of them will help you create a motivating commercial message. The fifth will help you establish a realistic marketing strategy. These elements are:

TARGET AUDIENCE
BENEFITS
COMPETITION
POSITIONING
MARKETING

In Section 1, I demonstrated a great system for identifying your Ideal Customer (Target Audience). In Section 3, I covered Committing to Your Specific Media (Marketing). And in Sections 4 & 5, I addressed Competition and Positioning.

In this Section, I will share with you techniques to create an effective message that will capture the attention of your ideal customers and motivate them to act--(Benefits).

What does an engaging advertisement look or sound like? How is it going to motivate the consumer audience? The following are four elements that should always be considered when you are creating an advertisement that grabs the consumer's attention.

INTRODUCTION
BRIDGE
OFFER
CLOSE

The Introduction is quite possibly the most important part of any advertisement. This is the advertiser's one shot at grabbing the consumer's attention before they move on to another opportunity. (Remember; refrain from using generic phrases or cliché opening statements).

The Introduction: Create one or two sentences that will grab the attention of your Ideal Customer.

_____

_____

_____

_____

_____

The second part of a well-crafted advertisement is ***The Bridge.*** Now that you have the attention of the audience, it's time to connect them to the body of your message. This is where you'll use one or two lines to bridge your Introduction to the Offer portion of your commercial.

The Bridge:

_____

_____

_____

_____

_____

The Offer is the heart of the message. This is where you present a strong, motivating reason for the audience to call your business. The key here is to make a compelling offer and highlight the benefit(s) of your product or service.

Start by asking yourself a few questions:

*What problem does your product or service solve?*_____

*Why do consumers buy your product or service?*_____

*What separates you from your competition?*_____

*Where does your business excel and why?*_____

The Offer:

_____

_____

_____

_____

(Remember: solve a problem for the consumer and they will respond to your advertisement)

This now brings us to our final element: *The Close*. This is where you tell the consumer how and where to contact your business. Again, keep this simple. Don't give the audience too many ways to reach you. It confuses the consumer and muddles the message.

The Close:

_____

_____

_____

_____

_____

PERSONAL NOTES

Section 3: Correcting the Third Mistake
The Guide to Committing to Your Specific Media
Corresponds with Chapter VI

Successful advertising campaigns, in part, are based on the selection of the right advertising media. If print medium is the right place to find your ideal customers, it's the right medium for your business.
Ask yourself the following questions to help you select the right media for your marketing campaign.

TELEVISION/CABLE:
YES   NO
Which Providers: _____

_____

Which Channels/Shows: _____

_____

_____

RADIO:
YES   NO
Which Stations/Deejays/Syndicated Shows: _____

_____

_____

PRINT:
YES   NO
Which Publications/Areas: _____

_____

_____

OUTDOOR/BILLBOARD:
YES   NO
Which Locations: _____

_____

_____

INTERNET/SOCIAL MEDIA:

YES   NO

Which Outlets: _____

_____

_____

DIRECT MAIL:

YES   NO

Which Geographic Locations: _____

_____

_____

GUERRILLA MARKETING:

YES   NO

Guerrilla Ideas or Suggestions: _____

_____

_____

EVENT MARKETING:

YES   NO

Type of Events: _____

_____

_____

Be sure to allow your campaign to breathe, and, over the course of time, you'll see your advertising efforts deliver amazing results. I recommend committing to a 13-week schedule as an absolute minimum for most advertising media. 26 weeks is ideal, but 13 weeks is the minimum. This will allow your message to build impressions and resonate with the audience; making a real impact on your ideal customers in the marketplace.

PERSONAL NOTES

Section 4: Correcting the Fourth Mistake
The Guide to Allocating a Proper Advertising Budget
Corresponds with Chapter VII

Consumers around the country continue to make large and small luxury purchases every day, as well as necessity purchases such as food, gas and clothing. Although we've all been told no one spends money when the economy is weakened, this is untrue. People are still spending, and they're doing so for a reason.

I cannot stress this next point enough: <u>Consumers never stop spending</u>, even during tough economic times. Consumers never stop spending. Spending may slow down, and consumers will make wiser purchasing decisions, but they never stop spending.

This is a critical point to understand. If consumers are making wise purchasing decisions, businesses must make wise advertising decisions to keep up with them. Just as consumers never stop spending, businesses cannot afford to stop advertising.

What percentage of your gross annual sales will be allocated to marketing?

3% = $ _____

7% = $ _____

10% = $ _____

15% = $ _____

Do you have Vendor/Co-op support dollars available?

$ _____

$ _____

$ _____

What does your business want to accomplish?
(Is it maintaining market share? Launching a new product line? Or is it just time to take the next step and establish your company as the industry leader?)

_____

_____

_____

_____

_____

Allocating your Annual Budget by Month
Jan. $ _____

Feb. $ _____

Mar. $ _____

Apr. $ _____

May $ _____

Jun. $ _____

Jul. $ _____

Aug. $ _____

Sept. $ _____

Oct. $ _____

Nov. $ _____

Dec. $ _____

Allocating your Media Marketing mix by Month (example: Radio, Print, Social Media)
Jan. _____

Feb. _____

Mar. _____

Apr. _____

May _____

Jun. _____

Jul. _____

Aug. _____

Sept. _____

Oct. _____

Nov. _____

Dec. _____

Here is one final thought on Allocating a Proper Advertising Budget...Without Breaking the Bank. The following is a quote from Charlie Mortimer, former head of General Foods. I think it sums up committing to a marketing budget quite brilliantly:

"The surest way to overspend on advertising is not to spend enough to do the job properly. It's like buying a ticket three-quarters of the way to Europe; you have spent some money, but you do not arrive."

PERSONAL NOTES

Section 5: Correcting the Fifth Mistake
The Guide to Enhancing Your Brand's Identity Through the
Power of Positioning
Corresponds with Chapter VIII

Many times consumers form an opinion of a business before they ever explore the company's products or services. Sometimes it can be as simple as the look of a building, or the name of a business, that turns a prospective consumer off. Other times it can be as subtle as the appearance of a company's website that pushes people away. Some of the smallest things can influence consumers to make an immediate decision about whether or not to become a customer. You need to stack the odds in your favor by creating a unique marketing position for your brand.

Positioning is about differentiating your brand in the minds of your ideal customers. It can turn people who are not currently patronizing your business into loyal customers for life.

When you properly position your brand, you'll build trust and credibility in the minds of your consumers.

While positioning is a common problem for many brands and businesses, the solution begins with the creation of a strong, identifying Competitive Advantage. There are two basic types of competitive advantage: *Cost Advantage* and *Differentiation Advantage*. They are defined as:

Cost Advantage:
Existing when a business is able to deliver the same benefits as competitors but at a lower cost.

Differentiation Advantage:
Delivering benefits that exceed those of competing products.

(Which one are you?)

Now, ask yourself the following questions.

How do you want to alter your brand's position?

_____

_____

_____

_____

How do you want to change the perception the marketplace may have already placed on your business?

_____

_____

_____

_____

(These answers are just the beginning to identifying
your brand's unique marketing position)

So, what is your business's Competitive Advantage? Is it Cost or Differentiation? Perhaps you are still unsure what your true competitive advantage is, and that's okay. Use the following questions to help you kick-start the dialog to create your competitive advantage.

What is your business's service or industry?

_____

_____

What are your profit centers?

_____

_____

What are your price points?

_____

_____

Is your business the recognized leader in your industry?

_____

_____

How much competition do you have in your industry?

_____

_____

Do you charge the lowest rate for products or services in your industry?

_____

_____

Does your business offer a unique product, service or material?

_____

_____

Who is your Ideal Customer?

_____

_____

What is the true benefit of your product or service to the consumer? (List two to three benefits)

_____

_____

What is it you're selling? A Product? Service? Quality? Lifestyle? Attitude? Idea? Solution?

_____

_____

Do you own a perception in the mind of your consumers?

_____

_____

What is the first thought or phrase you want consumers to think of when they hear the name of your business?

_____

_____

What do you love about your business that no one knows about?

_____

_____

What is the strength of your brand?

_____

_____

What is it about your business that keeps you up at night?

_____

_____

What is it about your marketing effort that keeps you up at night?

_____

_____

The whole idea of this exercise is to get you thinking about your brand's competitive advantage. Once your business identifies its competitive advantage, you must act on it. A business can achieve spectacular consumer growth once it identifies its unique position within the marketplace. A business's positioning becomes its identity, its battle cry. Best of all, it becomes the first thing consumers think of when they think of a business's product or service. (Remember: Be first in the consumer's mind).

Keep in mind, perception can become reality to consumers. So if you don't like the way the marketplace perceives your business, change it. Help consumers make a conscious and informed decision about your brand or business.

The marketplace may have the power to predetermine who you are, but ultimately you have the power to make the marketplace believe what you want them to through the Power of Positioning and the Power of Advertising.

PERSONAL NOTES

QUICK GLANCE MARKETING GRID

PROJECT/CAMPAIGN NAME

IDEAL CUSTOMER(S)

POSITIONING POINT

MEDIA MIX

MARKETING BUDGET

CORE SELLING MESSAGE

davidpetro|consulting

www.ingramcontent.com/pod-product-compliance
Lightning Source LLC
Chambersburg PA
CBHW071203220526
45468CB00003B/1144